THE TWISTED TALES

STAVYA GARG

Contents

Winner "GOLDEN BOOK AWARD 2024"
"NATIONAL PRIDE AWARD" winner for Youngest
Author of M.P. approved by Niti Ayog, Govt. of India.
Nominated as Youngest Fiction Author for-
India Book of Records (IBR)
Asia Book of Records (ABR)

Quick ! Thrilling readers,

**Sign here along with your address so that
everyone knows that this is your book !**

____

Foreword

Stavya is a prodigy! An International Olympiad Gold Medalist, vocalist, musician, doodler and what not and now a published author with so many laurels and awards in all fields....God Bless You !

Senior Journalist Mustafa Hussain, Voice of MP, Hindustan Times, PTI & News18India

Wavelength of storyline so full of mystery, suspense and heart pounding that it compelled me to finish the book in one night despite my busy schedule.

Ms. Ashmi Jain, Principal, TPGS, Neemuch

Lucid and Vivid enough description to keep authors bound...keep writing.

Dr. Vipul H. Garg, Senior Physician & Poet (father to Stavya)

I admire your expressive writing style and imagination, truly extraordinary..

Dr. Sonali Goyal, Gynaecologist & Obstetrician, first complete reader of the book.

Wonderful imagination and command on vocabulary, electrifying future, lots of love and best wishes...

Pooja Jain Jalori, Artist & Education Consultant

An amazing, engaging, well written book at such a young age, extremely talented..

Dr. Nidhi Pradhan, Gynaecologist & Obstetrician

Reading your book makes my day, Stavya, excited and proud of you...

Vaidehi Garg, student and avid reader.

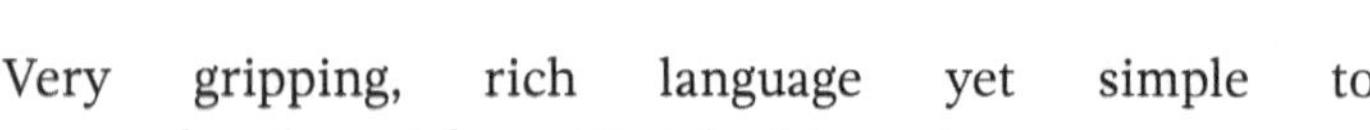

Very gripping, rich language yet simple to comprehend..eagerly waiting for his next...

Parshvi Jalori, Youngest author of millennium & IBR Awardee

Love you my son..keep going..long road to travel...

Dr. Shweta Garg, Paediatrician (mother to Stavya)

Acknowledgements

I would like to express my deepest gratitude to my family for their unwavering support throughout this writing journey. Their love, encouragement, and belief in my abilities have been a constant source of motivation. I am truly fortunate to have such a wonderful and understanding family.

In particular, I want to acknowledge my father, who has been my guiding light and source of inspiration. His unwavering belief in me and his constant encouragement have been instrumental in shaping my writing career. Thank you, Dad, for always pushing me to pursue my dreams.

I would also like to extend my heartfelt thanks to three remarkable authors who have had a profound impact on my writing. Chetan Bhagat, for his engaging storytelling and ability to connect with readers on a personal level. Ruskin Bond, for his enchanting tales that transport readers to a world of magic and wonder. And Paulo Coelho, for his thought-provoking and soul-stirring narratives that inspire introspection and self-discovery. Your works have been a constant source of inspiration, and I am grateful for the profound influence you have had on my writing.

Lastly, I want to extend my gratitude to all the readers who have taken the time to embark on this thrilling journey with me. Your support and enthusiasm for my work mean the world to me, and I am truly grateful for your presence on this literary adventure. Thank you all for being a part of this incredible journey. Without your support, this book would not have been possible.

Preface

I am an eleven year old boy (at the time when I am writing this book), so you must have got the idea that what I do throughout the day. I love reading and was recently focused on coding (Game Making). I always wanted to write a book like my favourite authors. I attended a workshop by Chetan Bhagat on writing, and that was when I started writing. I read "The Alchemist" by Paulo Coelho and thought that it would be great to write a book like that, so I started to write a book, but it was really hard to write a novel (especially when it has to be motivational like The Alchemist). After trying a ton of times, I could only write a incomplete book with 3 - 4 pages, that is when I thought that why shouldn't I write a book with short stories! I found out a book named "Musoorie Mystery" by Ruskin Bond. I got my inspiration and started writing a collection of thrillers, as my book is inspired by Ruskin Bond, you may find a few similarities.

I told my whole family about the book I am writing and everyone encouraged me especially my father, he told me that he is also writing an anthology and we together started working on our books. So, If you like-like poetry, be sure to check out "An Amalgam of a Doctor's

Intuitions" by my father.

So, at the end, I would like to say that just enjoy my book! I hope that you would love to read the thrillers that would put you at the edge of your seat.

A Note From The Author

Dear Reader,

Welcome to my thrilling collection of short stories! As the author, I am filled with excitement as I share this book with you. I wanted to take a moment to personally connect with you and share a few thoughts about this project.

First, I have always been captivated by the power of storytelling. The ability to transport readers into different worlds, to evoke emotions, and to keep them on the edge of their seats has always fascinated me. It was this passion for storytelling that inspired me to write this collection of thrilling short stories. I have always been an avid reader myself, constantly immersing myself in the pages of various books. The stories I read ignited my imagination and left me yearning to craft my own tales.

It was during one of these moments, when I found myself lost in the pages of another captivating novel, that the idea for this collection was born. I wanted to create a series of stories that would captivate readers in the same way, leaving them eagerly turning pages, hungry for more.

When I received the news that my book was going to be published, I was overjoyed. The feeling of being on cloud nine is an understatement. It was a moment of validation, a realization that my hard work and dedication had paid off. But more importantly, it was a reminder that dreams can come true if we believe in ourselves and pursue our passions relentlessly.

As you delve into the pages of this book, I hope you find yourself enthralled by the suspense, intrigued by the twists and turns, and compelled to keep reading until the very end. Each story has been carefully crafted to bring you suspense, mystery, and a touch of the unexpected. Beyond the thrills and chills, I also hope that this collection serves as an inspiration to you, the reader. Writing a book is not only a creative outlet but also a journey of self-discovery. It is my sincerest wish that these stories ignite a spark within you, encouraging you to explore your own storytelling abilities and perhaps even embark on your own writing journey.

Lastly, I want to express my gratitude to you, the reader. Without your support and curiosity, this book would not have come to fruition. It is because of readers like you that authors can continue to share their stories with the world, and for that, I am eternally grateful. So, buckle up and prepare to be taken on a thrilling ride through these pages. I hope you enjoy this collection as much as I enjoyed writing it. Remember, writing and publishing a book is an adventure like no other, and I am honored to have you join me on this journey. Happy reading !

Warm regards,
Stavya Garg

CHAPTER ONE

THE ENIGMA OF WHISPERING PINES

Once upon a time, in a small town called Whispering Pines, there was a mystery that had everyone talking. The townspeople were puzzled by strange occurrences that seemed to happen only at night. Whispers could be heard echoing through the trees, and eerie shadows danced in the moonlight.

The story began when a young girl named Lily moved to Whispering Pines with her family. She was twelve years old and full of curiosity. Lily loved exploring and had a knack for solving puzzles. As soon as she heard about the enigma of Whispering Pines, she couldn't resist digging deeper.

One moonlit night, Lily decided to investigate the whispers for herself. She snuck out of her house, flashlight in hand, and made her way to the edge of the mysterious forest. As she entered the woods, the trees seemed to whisper secrets to her, urging her forward.

Lily followed the whispers until she stumbled upon an old abandoned mansion. The mansion was rumored to be haunted, but Lily wasn't easily scared. She approached the creaking front door and pushed it open, revealing a dimly lit hallway.

As Lily ventured further into the mansion, she noticed strange symbols etched into the walls. They seemed to be a secret code, and Lily's eyes lit up with excitement. She took out her notebook and began deciphering the symbols, determined to uncover the truth.

With each symbol she decoded, Lily grew more intrigued. The whispers grew louder, guiding her to a hidden room. Inside, she found a dusty old book that held the answers she had been seeking. The book revealed a dark secret about Whispering Pines.

Long ago, a powerful sorcerer had inhabited the town. He had used his magic to create an enchanted forest, but his powers had become corrupted. The sorcerer's spirit was trapped in the forest, and his whispers were a cry for help.

Lily realized that the only way to free the sorcerer's spirit was to gather special artifacts hidden throughout the town. Each artifact held a piece of the sorcerer's magic, and when combined, they could break the enchantment.

Lily embarked on a quest to find the artifacts, enlisting the help of her newfound friends in Whispering Pines. Together, they braved many challenges and solved numerous riddles to collect the artifacts. With each artifact they found, the whispers grew weaker, and the forest began to lose its eerie aura.

Along their journey, Lily and her friends encountered various obstacles. They faced treacherous paths guarded by mythical creatures, solved intricate puzzles in ancient ruins, and even ventured into the depths of an underground labyrinth. Each challenge tested their courage, intelligence, and teamwork.

As they continued their quest, Lily and her friends discovered more about the history of Whispering Pines. They learned that the sorcerer's enchantment had not only trapped his spirit but also affected the entire town. The once vibrant community had become isolated and fearful, with the townspeople living in constant unease.

Determined to restore harmony to Whispering Pines, Lily and her friends delved deeper into the sorcerer's past. They uncovered tales of his benevolence before his powers were corrupted, and stories of his deep connection to the enchanted forest. Through their research, they discovered that the artifacts they sought were scattered across Whispering Pines, hidden in places of significance to the sorcerer.

As Lily and her friends ventured through the town, they encountered unique challenges in each location. At the Whispering Willow Park, they had to solve a riddle hidden within the playground equipment to retrieve an ancient amulet. In the Whispering Caves, they navigated a maze of winding tunnels, avoiding traps, and retrieving a magical crystal.

With each artifact they collected, the townspeople's hope began to rekindle. Whispers of gratitude and encouragement replaced the haunting whispers of the sorcerer. The once gloomy streets of Whispering Pines slowly regained their vibrancy as the enchantment weakened.

However, the sorcerer was not willing to give up easily. As Lily and her friends neared their final artifact, they faced their greatest challenge yet. The sorcerer, in a last attempt to maintain control, unleashed his most powerful magic to stop them. The town was shrouded in darkness, and the whispers grew louder and more menacing.

But Lily and her friends refused to be deterred. They relied on their friendship, unwavering determination, and the knowledge they had gained throughout their journey. With a combined effort, they channeled their inner strength and overcame the sorcerer's final obstacle, acquiring the last artifact.

With all the artifacts in their possession, Lily and her friends returned to the abandoned mansion. They created a sacred circle, placing the artifacts in the center. As they chanted an ancient incantation, a brilliant light enveloped the room, dispersing the darkness that had plagued the town.

The sorcerer's spirit was finally released, free from the corruption that had bound him for centuries. He appeared before Lily and her friends, his form ethereal yet grateful. He expressed his gratitude for their courage and determination, acknowledging that they had not only saved him but also restored the balance of Whispering Pines.

As a token of his gratitude, the sorcerer bestowed upon Lily and her friends a gift. He granted them a small portion of his magic, allowing them to keep a connection to the enchanted forest and continue protecting the town from any future threats.

Whispering Pines was forever changed by Lily and her friends' heroic actions. The town flourished, and the once divided townspeople came together to celebrate their newfound unity. The whispers that had once haunted the town transformed into joyous laughter and heartfelt conversations.

Lily and her friends became local heroes, their names forever engraved in the history of Whispering Pines. They continued their adventures, using their newfound magic and friendship to help others in need. And as for Whispering Pines, it remained a place of wonder and enchantment, reminding all who visited of the power of belief, courage, and the triumph of good over evil.

And so, the enigma of Whispering Pines became a legendary tale passed down from generation to generation, a reminder of the extraordinary journey that began with a curious girl named Lily and her friends. Their story would forever inspire others to embrace their own inner strength and embark on their own adventures, knowing that even the most mysterious of challenges could be overcome with determination and a little bit of magic.

With the enchantment broken and the town of Whispering Pines restored to its former glory, Lily and her friends found themselves at a crossroads. The adventures they had embarked on had changed them, and they yearned for more excitement and the opportunity to help others. They were determined to use their newfound magic and friendship to make a difference in the world.

As they gathered in their secret meeting spot, a cozy treehouse nestled in the heart of the enchanted forest, Lily proposed an idea. "What if we become a team of adventurers, traveling far and wide to help those in need?" she suggested, her eyes sparkling with excitement.

Her friends, Ethan, Maya, and Alex, all agreed wholeheartedly. They had formed an unbreakable bond during their quest to free the sorcerer's spirit, and they couldn't imagine a better way to spend their days than exploring new places and using their magical abilities for good.

And so, the Whispering Pines Adventure Club was born. Lily, the fearless leader, brought her sharp intellect and problem-solving skills. Ethan, with his strength and unwavering determination, became the group's protector. Maya, with her keen intuition and connection to nature, became the group's guide. And Alex, with his quick wit and ability to think on his feet, became the group's strategist.

Their first mission took them to a distant land, where a village was plagued by a wicked sorceress who had seized control of their river, causing a drought that threatened their crops and livelihoods. The villagers had heard of the Whispering Pines Adventure Club and sent a desperate plea for help.

Upon arriving in the village, the adventurers were greeted with gratitude and hope. The villagers shared stories of the sorceress's reign and the hardships they had endured. Lily and her friends knew they needed to act quickly to restore balance to the land.

They set out to investigate the source of the sorceress's power, traversing treacherous terrain and facing magical creatures sent to guard her domain. With their combined strength and magical abilities, they overcame each obstacle, inching closer to their ultimate goal.

Finally, they reached the heart of the sorceress's lair, a towering castle surrounded by dark clouds and swirling mists. Inside, they encountered enchanted traps and illusions designed to test their resolve. But the adventurers relied on their trust in one another and their unwavering determination to press forward.

As they confronted the sorceress, a fierce battle ensued. The sorceress unleashed her dark magic, attempting to overpower the adventurers. But Lily and her friends stood firm, using their combined abilities and teamwork to weaken her defenses.

In a climactic final showdown, Lily channeled her inner strength and tapped into the sorcerer's magic bestowed upon her. With a burst of light, she cast a powerful spell that broke the sorceress's hold on the river, allowing its waters to flow freely once again.

The villagers rejoiced as the river returned to its full glory, bringing life back to their crops and rejuvenating their spirits. They celebrated the Whispering Pines Adventure Club as heroes, forever grateful for their selfless act.

Word of their heroic deeds spread far and wide, and soon, the adventurers found themselves in high demand. They received requests for assistance from all corners of the realm, from villages plagued by dark creatures to kingdoms threatened by evil forces. Each mission brought its own unique challenges and dangers, but the Whispering Pines Adventure Club faced them head-on, bringing hope and light wherever they went.

Along their journey, they encountered a wide array of magical beings and made new allies. They met wise old wizards who shared their knowledge, mischievous fairies who provided helpful tricks, and noble knights who fought alongside them. These encounters enriched their experiences and expanded their understanding of the magical world they had become a part of.

As the Whispering Pines Adventure Club continued their noble quest, they never forgot their roots. They returned to Whispering Pines whenever they could, using their magic to protect the town and ensure its continued prosperity. The townspeople, forever grateful for their bravery, welcomed them with open arms and celebrated their achievements.

But amidst their adventures, the adventurers never lost sight of their friendship and the bond that had brought them together. In moments of respite, they would gather in their treehouse, sharing stories and laughter, cherishing the memories they had created.

In time, the Whispering Pines Adventure Club became legends in their own right. Songs were sung about their bravery, and children aspired to be like them. Their impact on the world was immeasurable, and their legacy lived on through the stories told for generations to come.

And so, the adventures of Lily, Ethan, Maya, and Alex continued, as they traversed the realms, seeking new challenges and helping those in need. They embraced the unknown, knowing that with their friendship and magic, they could overcome any obstacle.

For the Whispering Pines Adventure Club, the world was their playground, and together, they would leave a trail of hope and magic wherever they went. And in their hearts, they carried the spirit of Whispering Pines, forever grateful for the town that had sparked their incredible journey and forever bound by the unbreakable bond they had formed.

CHAPTER TWO

DEATH OF SAMUEL TAYLOR

In the quiet town of Tandermuk, a thick fog settled over the streets. The townspeople went about their daily lives,under to the dark cloud that loomed over their quaint community.

One evening, the lifeless body of Mr. Samuel Taylor, a local businessman, was discovered in his old mansion. The news spread through Tandermuk like a lightning, sending thoughts of fear and suspicion among its inhabitants.

Detective Flint arrived at the crime scene, his eyes scanning the room for any trace of evidence. The air was heavy with fear, as the detective took a dive in the life of Mr. Taylor and the secrets that lay hidden beneath the surface.

As Flint continued to investigate the suspicious life, he discovered a lot of leads which say opposite things making him more confused. Each suspect seemed suspicious with secrets hidden inside them.

Among the suspect was Mrs. Diana Keen, Mr. Taylor's business partner, who had a long story and relation with Mr. Taylor and was one of the most doubtful. Then there was Matthew Taylor, the greedy son, who had a desire to take over all the fortune of his father. Lastly, there was Ms. Victoria Harper, a dark and mysterious artist with deep darkness, whose dark and silent paintings seemed to tell the tragedy that had once taken place in Tandermuk.

As Flint curiously pieced together the puzzle of the investigation, he got a confusion upon a series of unsolved murders that had haunted the town's history. The echoes of the past murders echoed in the present, sending chills down the detective's spine as he realized that there there was a link that connected these acts.

Time seemed to slip through Flint's as he raced against the clock, he had a lot of things to uncover but had a very little time. In his search of the truth, he discovered a hidden diary belonging to Mr. Taylor, its pages filled with confusing entries and notes. The diary had the key that could open the book containing all secrets of his life, maybe even his death.

He found out the killer from the leads, he was nobody else but Charles Cooper,he confessed everything and told something that told that why hundreds of people died in the town, he belonged to a family who have killed almost a hundred people of this town from past to present. Suddenly his breath became heavy and he died there with a heart attack.

With the killer died, Tanderwood breathed a sigh of relief. The echoes of darkness that had gripped the community began to fade, replaced by a renewed sense of security.

As time passed, the echoes of the murder mystery lingered in the wind, carried on the whispers of the townsfolk. The memory of the dark days served as a stark reminder of the fragility of trust and the depths of darkness that could reside within one's own heart.

While interrogating the suspects, Flint discovered that Mrs. Diana Keen had a secret friend, Mr. Jonathan Redington, a lawyer in Tandermuk. They revealed a motive for both of them to eliminate Mr. Taylor, as they wanted to take control of his business empire. Charles Cooper worked for Diana and whatever he said was lie.

But just as Flint thought he had cracked the case, a mysterious person was found known as "The Whisper," this individual knew everything about everyone in Tandermuk. The Whisper followed Flint, leaving cryptic messages and clues that hinted at a much larger mystery.

As Flint followed the trail left by The Whisper, he discovered a hidden underground society operating under the town. This secret organization, known as "The Shadows," having ultimate power and influence, manipulating events for their own gain. Mr. Taylor's murder was just a pawn in their grand scheme.

With time running out, Flint found himself caught in a deadly game of cat and mouse with The Whisper and The Shadows. Each step closer to the truth brought him closer to danger, as he realized that the true mastermind behind the murder was someone he never expected.

With his investigation on Shadows, it was revealed that Matthew Taylor, the greedy son, had planned his father's murder. Motivated by years of neglect, Matthew had joined The Shadows, using their resources and influence to carry out his plan for revenge.

Flint, now faced with the task of bringing dow both The Shadows and Matthew, had to navigate a confusing web of darkness and confusion. It became a race against time to expose the truth, protect innocent lives, and bring justice to Tandermuk.

Flint confronted Matthew, unraveling the layers of his twisted plot. But just as justice seemed within reach, The Whisper, the enigmatic figure who had haunted Flint throughout the investigation, vanished without a trace.

As the dust settled in Tandermuk, the town slowly began to heal from the wounds inflicted by The Shadows and Matthew's terror. Flint, forever marked by the darkness he had uncovered, continued his work as a detective, vowing to keep Tandermuk safe from the shadows that lurked beneath its surface.

But deep within the hearts of the townsfolk, the whispers of The Whisper remained, a constant reminder that even in the lightest of places, darkness could still be born. And Detective Flint knew that his battle against the shadows was far from over.

CHAPTER THREE

JONATHAN'S MYSTERIOUS ADVENTURE

Jonathan was an ordinary boy with a big imagination. He loved to explore and find new adventures. One sunny day, while he was walking through the forest near his house, he found a hidden path. He decided to follow it and see where it led.

As he walked along the winding path, Jonathan noticed the air getting cooler and the sounds of nature getting quieter. He felt excited and wondered what he would find. Suddenly, the path opened up to a beautiful clearing with a sparkling waterfall flowing into a clear pool.

Jonathan was amazed at the sight before him. He couldn't resist dipping his toes into the cool water. But as he did, something magical happened. The water glowed, and Jonathan felt a strange tingling feeling all over his body.

Out of the pool emerged a wise old wizard named Merlin. He had a long white beard and twinkling eyes.

"Welcome, young adventurer," Merlin greeted Jonathan. "You have found a secret portal to enchanted lands. I have been waiting for someone like you to discover it."

Jonathan's heart raced with excitement. He couldn't believe his luck. "What kind of enchanted lands are there?" he asked, curious.

Merlin smiled kindly. "There are many magical places to explore. But be careful, not all of them are friendly. You must be brave and make wise choices. Are you ready for this extraordinary journey?"

Jonathan nodded without hesitation. He had always dreamed of going on a grand adventure, and this was his chance.

"Very well," Merlin said. "But before you go, I must give you a special gift." He took out a small, shiny amulet from his robe. "This amulet is powerful. It will guide and protect you on your journey. Wear it always and trust in its magic."

Jonathan eagerly took the amulet and put it around his neck. He could feel its energy and felt more confident.

"Now, my young friend," Merlin continued, "choose your first destination. I will send you to a land of ancient mysteries and hidden treasures."

Jonathan thought for a moment, his mind racing with ideas. Finally, he made up his mind. "I choose the Land of Whispers," he declared.

Merlin nodded approvingly. "A good choice, Jonathan. The Land of Whispers is a place where secrets hide. But remember, not all whispers are meant to be heard. Be careful and trust your instincts."

With a wave of his hand, Merlin cast a spell, and Jonathan felt himself being transported to a world he could never have imagined.

When he arrived in the Land of Whispers, Jonathan felt a strange silence. The air was heavy, and he had a feeling that he was not alone. As he cautiously moved forward, he noticed a strange stone tablet covered in old writing.

Curiosity got the better of him, and Jonathan touched the tablet. Suddenly, the words on it started to glow, and a voice filled the air. "To discover the secrets of this land, you must solve the riddles hidden within."

Jonathan's eyes widened with excitement. He loved solving puzzles and riddles. This was his chance to put his skills to the test.

For days and nights, Jonathan explored the Land of Whispers, solving riddles and finding hidden clues. Each riddle brought him closer to the heart of the land, where a priceless treasure awaited him.

But as Jonathan delved deeper into the mysteries of the land, he faced challenges and dangers he hadn't expected. Dark creatures lurked in the shadows, ready to attack. The whispers grew louder and more dangerous, trying to lead him astray.

Yet, Jonathan didn't give up. With the help of his amulet and the wisdom he gained from Merlin, he navigated treacherous landscapes and outsmarted cunning opponents.

Finally, after days of difficult exploration, Jonathan reached the heart of the land. The treasure he had been searching for was within his reach. But as he reached out to take it, a voice echoed through the chamber.

"Congratulations, young Jonathan," the voice said. "You have proven yourself worthy. But remember, the real treasures are not material things, but the lessons you learn and the friends you make along the way."

Jonathan paused and thought about the words. He realized that his journey was about more than just finding a treasure. It was about finding his own strength and the joy of exploring.

With a new understanding, Jonathan left the Land of Whispers, saying goodbye to the mysteries that had captivated him. He returned to his normal life, forever changed by the extraordinary adventure he had experienced.

From that day forward, Jonathan continued to explore the world around him, knowing that there were always new adventures waiting. With his amulet as a reminder of the magic in the world, he embarked on new journeys, eager to uncover the secrets hidden in the whispers of the unknown.

CHAPTER FOUR

MYSTERIOUS GIFTS

Max was an ordinary boy with an extraordinary curiosity. He loved to explore the world around him and discover new things. One sunny afternoon, as Max was playing in his backyard, he noticed a peculiar package sitting on his doorstep. It was wrapped in beautiful, shimmering paper, and a note attached to it read, "For Max, the curious adventurer."

Intrigued, Max tore open the package and found a small, intricately carved wooden box inside. With trembling hands, he opened the box and gasped in astonishment. Inside were three mysterious gifts - a silver compass, a delicate glass bottle, and a small leather-bound journal.

Max's heart raced with excitement. He couldn't wait to uncover the secrets these gifts held. With the gifts in his possession, Max decided to embark on an adventure to unravel their mysteries.

He started with the silver compass. As he held it in his hand, the needle began to spin wildly. Max followed its erratic movements and soon found himself standing at the entrance of an ancient, overgrown forest.

With the compass as his guide, Max ventured into the forest, its lush greenery and towering trees enveloping him. As he walked deeper into the woods, he noticed a soft glow emanating from a grove of trees. Curiosity getting the better of him, Max followed the glow and stumbled upon a hidden clearing.

In the center of the clearing stood a magnificent tree, its branches reaching towards the sky. Hanging from the branches were sparkling crystals, each reflecting a different color of the rainbow. Max marveled at the sight, feeling a sense of awe and wonder.

As he approached the tree, a gentle voice whispered in his ear, "Young adventurer, you have found the Tree of Dreams. Each crystal holds a dream waiting to be fulfilled. Choose wisely, for the dreams you select will shape your journey."

Max carefully examined the crystals, each one shimmering with its unique allure. After much contemplation, he chose a deep blue crystal, drawn to its calming energy. As he held it in his hand, he felt a surge of inspiration and determination.

With the blue crystal in his pocket, Max continued his adventure, guided by the compass once again. He soon found himself standing at the edge of a vast, sparkling lake. The glass bottle in his hand seemed to whisper, urging him to explore its depths.

Max took a deep breath and plunged into the crystal-clear waters. As he swam deeper, he discovered a hidden underwater kingdom, teeming with vibrant coral reefs and playful sea creatures. He marveled at the beauty that surrounded him, feeling a deep connection to the ocean.

In the heart of the kingdom, he encountered a wise mermaid who spoke in gentle tones. "Welcome, young adventurer. You have found the Realm of Wishes. Each creature here holds a wish, waiting to be granted. Choose one wish and use it wisely."

Max swam alongside the mermaid, observing the sea creatures and listening to their wishes. After much consideration, he decided to grant the wish of a lonely seahorse who longed for companionship.

With a touch of his hand, Max granted the seahorse's wish, and in an instant, a playful school of seahorses appeared, bringing joy and laughter to the lonely creature. Max felt a sense of fulfillment and happiness, knowing he had made a difference in someone's life.

Leaving the underwater kingdom behind, Max continued his journey, guided by the compass and the glass bottle. The final gift, the leather-bound journal, held the key to his next destination.

As Max opened the journal, he found that its pages were blank, waiting to be filled with his own stories and adventures. With a sense of excitement, he began to write, capturing the memories and lessons he had learned along the way.

With each word he penned, Max's imagination soared, and the stories seemed to come alive on the pages. He wrote of his encounters with the Tree of Dreams, the underwater kingdom, and the wishes he had granted. The journal became a treasure trove of his experiences, a testament to his journey as a curious adventurer.

As Max reached the end of his journal, he realized that the true gift lay not in the objects themselves but in the experiences and lessons they had brought him. The compass had guided him to the Tree of Dreams, where he learned the importance of choosing his path wisely. The glass bottle had led him to the underwater kingdom, where he discovered the power of granting wishes. And the journal had allowed him to capture and share his adventures, creating memories that would last a lifetime.

With a newfound wisdom and a heart full of gratitude, Max returned home, cherishing the mysterious gifts that had transformed his life. He knew that his curiosity would continue to lead him on new journeys, and he eagerly awaited the next chapter of his adventures.

Days turned into weeks, and weeks turned into months. Max's passion for adventure remained strong, and he found himself yearning for new discoveries. One morning, as he was exploring the attic, he stumbled upon an old map tucked away in a dusty corner.

The map showed a hidden island, rumored to hold ancient treasures and untold mysteries. Max's eyes gleamed with excitement as he studied the map, tracing the winding paths and hidden landmarks. He knew that this was his next great adventure.

Gathering his compass, glass bottle, and journal, Max set out on a journey to find the hidden island. The compass pointed him in the right direction, guiding him through treacherous waters and uncharted territories. With each passing day, his anticipation grew, fueled by the unknown that awaited him.

After weeks of sailing, Max spotted a speck of land on the horizon. As he approached, the island revealed itself in all its splendor - lush forests, towering mountains, and pristine beaches. It was a paradise untouched by time.

Eager to explore, Max stepped onto the island's shores. With the compass in hand, he navigated through the dense foliage, his senses heightened by the unfamiliar sounds and scents of the island. Every step brought him closer to the heart of the island, where he hoped to uncover its hidden treasures.

As he ventured deeper, Max stumbled upon a crumbling temple, its walls adorned with ancient symbols and intricate carvings. The glass bottle in his hand seemed to vibrate with anticipation, urging him to enter the temple and discover its secrets.

With cautious steps, Max entered the temple, the air thick with a sense of mystery and reverence. He followed a dimly lit corridor, his heart pounding with excitement. At the end of the corridor, he found a chamber filled with glowing crystals, illuminating the room with a soft, ethereal light.

In the center of the chamber stood a pedestal, upon which rested a single, radiant crystal. Max approached it, his hand trembling with anticipation. As he touched the crystal, a surge of energy coursed through his body, filling him with a profound sense of purpose.

A voice echoed through the chamber, ancient and wise. "Max, the seeker of knowledge, you have uncovered the Crystal of Wisdom. It holds the collective knowledge of the island, waiting to be unlocked. Seek the answers you seek, and let the wisdom guide you in your path."

Max closed his eyes, allowing the energy of the crystal to envelop him. Visions flashed before his eyes - images of forgotten civilizations, ancient rituals, and untold stories. He felt a deep connection to the island, as if its history and wisdom were now a part of him.

With the newfound knowledge, Max emerged from the temple, his mind buzzing with possibilities. He knew that the island held more secrets to be discovered, and he was determined to uncover them all.

Days turned into weeks, and weeks turned into months as Max explored every nook and cranny of the island. He discovered hidden caves filled with sparkling gemstones, ancient ruins that told stories of lost civilizations, and breathtaking vistas that took his breath away.

With each discovery, Max recorded his experiences in his journal, capturing the essence of the island and the wisdom he had gained. The journal became a testament to his growth as an adventurer, a chronicle of the lessons learned and the challenges overcome.

As he delved deeper into the mysteries of the island, Max encountered a group of friendly island dwellers - a community that had made the island their home for generations. They welcomed him with open arms, eager to share their stories and wisdom.

Through their guidance, Max learned about the island's rich history and the customs of its inhabitants. He participated in their rituals, listened to their legends, and even learned their traditional dances. The island became more than just a place of adventure; it became a second home, filled with warmth and camaraderie.

One evening, as Max sat around a bonfire with the islanders, an elder shared a tale of a legendary treasure hidden deep within the island. It was said to possess unimaginable power - the power to grant any wish, to heal any wound, and to bring harmony to the world.

Max's heart raced with excitement. He knew that this was his ultimate quest, the culmination of all his adventures. With the islanders' support, he set out to find the legendary treasure, guided by the compass, glass bottle, and journal that had brought him this far.

The journey was treacherous, filled with perilous cliffs, dense jungles, and hidden traps. But Max pressed on, fueled by his determination and the belief that the treasure held the key to a better world.

After days of navigating through the island's most challenging terrain, Max found himself standing at the entrance of a hidden cave. The compass pointed towards it, urging him to enter. With a deep breath, he stepped into the darkness, his heart pounding with anticipation.

Inside the cave, Max discovered a vast chamber, illuminated by a soft, golden light. In the center of the chamber stood a magnificent pedestal, upon which rested a glowing orb. It pulsed with a gentle energy, as if it held everything Max wanted or needed, and it did.

CHAPTER FIVE

CONFUSION OF EVERMORE

Once upon a time, in the quaint town of Evermore, there lived a renowned archaeologist named Alexander Reed. Known for his expertise in uncovering ancient secrets, Alexander was a man of great curiosity and adventure. His reputation had spread far and wide, and he had become a legend in his own right.

One fateful evening, Alexander arrived in Evermore, drawn to the town by a rumor that whispered of a hidden artifact, said to possess unimaginable power. The townspeople were abuzz with excitement and intrigue at the arrival of such a distinguished explorer.

Among the curious locals was Amelia Hartley, a young and aspiring journalist with a passion for uncovering the truth. Determined to get the scoop on Alexander's mission, she set out to interview him and discover the secrets that lay within Evermore's borders.

Amelia found Alexander engrossed in ancient scrolls and maps at a local café. Intrigued by his intense focus, she approached him and introduced herself. Recognizing Amelia's passion for the truth, Alexander agreed to share his story.

He revealed that he had stumbled upon an ancient legend that spoke of a powerful artifact hidden deep within the enchanted forest surrounding Evermore. This artifact, according to the legend, was said to possess the ability to grant immense power to its wielder, but it had been lost for centuries.

Eager to unravel the mystery and uncover the truth, Amelia offered her assistance to Alexander. Together, they delved into the town's history, piecing together clues and deciphering cryptic symbols. As they dug deeper, they discovered that the artifact was not just a legend but a tangible reality that had the potential to change the course of history.

Unbeknownst to Alexander and Amelia, their investigation had not gone unnoticed. A dark and sinister organization known as the Shadow Syndicate had been monitoring their every move. Led by the enigmatic and ruthless Damien Crule, the Shadow Syndicate sought to obtain the artifact for their own nefarious purposes.

Undeterred by the looming threat, Alexander and Amelia continued their search. They uncovered a hidden chamber beneath an ancient oak tree in the heart of the forest. Inside, they found a map leading to the artifact's location - a long-forgotten temple hidden deep within the mountains.

Excitement surged through their veins as they embarked on the perilous journey to the temple. Along the way, they encountered treacherous terrain, cunning traps, and riddles that tested their wits. It was a race against time, as they knew the Shadow Syndicate was hot on their heels.

Finally, after days of arduous travel, Alexander and Amelia reached the temple. Its majestic facade loomed before them, ancient and weathered. As they stepped inside, they marveled at the intricate carvings and ornate statues that adorned the walls.

Navigating the temple's labyrinthine corridors, they encountered mythical creatures guarding the artifact. With their combined knowledge and bravery, they overcame each challenge, inching closer to their goal.

Just as Alexander and Amelia reached the inner sanctum, the Shadow Syndicate caught up to them. Damien Crule, his eyes filled with malevolence, confronted them with a wicked smile.

"You've walked right into my trap," he sneered. "Hand over the artifact, or suffer the consequences."

Unyielding, Alexander and Amelia refused to back down. They knew that the artifact's power must not fall into the wrong hands. A fierce battle ensued, as they fought against the Shadow Syndicate's minions, their determination unwavering.

In a climactic moment, Alexander and Amelia managed to defeat Damien Crule. With the Shadow Syndicate defeated, they turned their attention to the artifact. As they approached it, a surge of energy enveloped the room, radiating with ancient power.

With trepidation, they reached out and touched the artifact, unlocking its true potential. A blinding light filled the room as the artifact unleashed its power, not in destruction, but in a wave of healing and renewal.

As the light faded, Alexander and Amelia stood in awe, witnessing the transformation that had occurred. The artifact had not only granted immense power but had also restored balance and harmony to Evermore and its surrounding lands.

Grateful for their role in this extraordinary journey, the townspeople of Evermore hailed Alexander and Amelia as heroes. They celebrated their triumph, recognizing the importance of their unwavering dedication to the truth.

In the aftermath, Alexander and Amelia decided to stay in Evermore, using their newfound knowledge and experience to protect the town from future threats. They formed an alliance, vowing to uncover hidden truths, expose corruption, and ensure the safety of their beloved town.

And so, Alexander Reed and Amelia Hartley became the guardians of Evermore, forever linked by the enigma they had unraveled and the bond they had forged in the face of darkness. Together, they would continue to explore the mysteries of the world, their adventures becoming legendary tales passed down through generations.

Years passed, and Evermore thrived under the watchful eyes of Alexander and Amelia. However, whispers of a new threat began to circulate. Rumors spoke of a secret society, even more dangerous than the Shadow Syndicate, seeking to harness the power of the artifact for their own sinister purposes.

The society, known as the Order of Shadows, was led by a mysterious figure named Damien Crule. Unbeknownst to Alexander and Amelia, Damien had survived their previous encounter and had become obsessed with obtaining the artifact.

Determined to protect Evermore, Alexander and Amelia embarked on a new quest to uncover the truth behind the Order of Shadows and their plans. They journeyed to distant lands, gathering information and enlisting the help of allies along the way.

Their investigation led them to ancient libraries, hidden temples, and forgotten ruins. They deciphered ancient texts, piecing together the history of the Order and its connection to the artifact. They discovered that the Order believed the artifact held the key to unlocking ultimate power and domination over the world.

As Alexander and Amelia delved deeper into the secrets of the Order, they realized that the artifact's true purpose was not just to grant power but to maintain the delicate balance between light and darkness. It was a beacon of hope, meant to ensure that no single entity could wield unchecked power.

Armed with this knowledge, Alexander and Amelia rallied the people of Evermore and formed an alliance with other towns and nations. They prepared for an epic battle against the Order of Shadows, knowing that the fate of their world hung in the balance.

The final confrontation took place in the heart of Evermore, where the Order had gathered to claim the artifact. The battle raged, with Alexander and Amelia leading the charge against Damien Crule and his minions.

It was a battle of epic proportions, with magic and steel clashing in a symphony of chaos. The townspeople fought valiantly alongside Alexander and Amelia, their determination fueled by the desire to protect their home and preserve the balance.

In a climactic moment, Alexander faced Damien Crule in a one-on-one duel. Their swords clashed, each strike resonating with the weight of their convictions. The fight was fierce and intense, as both combatants pushed their limits.

Finally, with a final strike, Alexander disarmed Damien and delivered a decisive blow. Damien Crule, defeated and broken, fell to the ground. The Order of Shadows, without its leader, crumbled, their plans thwarted.

The artifact, now safe and secure, emitted a radiant light, signifying the restoration of balance and harmony to the world. Evermore rejoiced, celebrating the victory over the forces of darkness and the preservation of their way of life.

Alexander and Amelia, hailed as heroes once again, knew that their journey was far from over. They vowed to remain vigilant, protecting Evermore and the world from any future threats. Their legacy of bravery and unwavering dedication to the truth would continue to inspire generations to come.

And so, Alexander Reed and Amelia Hartley, the guardians of Evermore, embarked on a new chapter of their lives, forever linked by their shared adventures, their unyielding bond, and their commitment to the greater good. Together, they would face whatever challenges awaited them, knowing that their courage and determination would always prevail.

CHAPTER SIX

SLEEPY SMOKE

Once upon a time in the small town of Sleepy Hollow, there was a mysterious occurrence known as the Sleepy Smoke. It was said that every night at midnight, a thick fog would roll into town, enveloping the streets and houses in a dense cloud of smoke. The Sleepy Smoke had a peculiar effect on the townspeople. As soon as they inhaled its fumes, they would become drowsy and fall into a deep sleep.

No one knew where the smoke came from or why it had such an effect, but the residents of Sleepy Hollow lived in fear of its arrival each night. One night, a young detective named Jack arrived in Sleepy Hollow to investigate the phenomenon. Armed with nothing but his wits and a determination to uncover the truth, Jack set out to unravel the mystery behind the Sleepy Smoke.

As midnight approached, Jack positioned himself in the town square, waiting for the smoke to appear. Sure enough, as the clock struck twelve, a thick fog began to creep through the streets, swirling and twirling like an eerie dance. Jack held his breath, not wanting to succumb to the smoke's sleepy spell. With a flashlight in hand, Jack ventured into the smoke-filled streets, his heart pounding in his chest.

He followed the trail of smoke, weaving through the deserted town. The air was heavy with a silence, broken only by the sound of his own footsteps. As he delved deeper into the mist, Jack stumbled upon an old, abandoned factory. The smoke seemed to be emanating from within its crumbling walls. Curiosity and determination fueled his every step as he cautiously entered the building.

Inside, Jack discovered a hidden laboratory. Beakers and test tubes lined the shelves, filled with strange chemicals. It became clear that someone had been experimenting with the Sleepy Smoke, harnessing its power for their own purposes. Suddenly, a figure emerged from the shadows, in a cloak. It was the mastermind behind the Sleepy Smoke - Dr. Blackwood, a brilliant but twisted scientist.

He revealed his sinister plan to use the smoke to control the minds of the townspeople, bending them to his will. Jack knew he had to stop Dr. Blackwood before it was too late. A fierce battle started, with Jack dodging the smoke-filled attacks and fighting back with strength he possessed.

The room was engulfed in chaos as glass shattered and chemicals spilled. In a final, desperate move, Jack managed to knock Dr. Blackwood unconscious, putting an end to his villainous scheme. The Sleepy Smoke ended, leaving the town of Sleepy Hollow free from its spell.

The townspeople awoke, unaware of the danger they had been in. Jack was hailed as a hero, praised for his bravery and quick thinking. As he left Sleepy Hollow, he knew that he had made a difference, protecting the innocent from the clutches of evil. And so, the Sleepy Smoke became nothing more than a distant memory in the town of Sleepy Hollow, a reminder of the darkness that had once threatened to consume it. Jack continued his detective work, knowing that there were always new mysteries to uncover and battles to be fought.

As Jack left Sleepy Hollow, he couldn't shake the feeling that there was more to the Sleepy Smoke than he had uncovered. He couldn't simply walk away, leaving the town vulnerable to the possibility of another villain rising to power. Driven by his insatiable curiosity and determination, Jack decided to return to Sleepy Hollow.

He knew he had to dig deeper into the origins of the Sleepy Smoke and ensure that no remnants of Dr. Blackwood's sinister plans remained. Upon his return, Jack began to investigate the abandoned factory further. He meticulously examined the laboratory, searching for any clues or hidden documents that could shed light on the true nature of the Sleepy Smoke.

Days turned into nights as Jack tirelessly combed through the remnants of Dr. Blackwood's experiments. Finally, he stumbled upon a hidden compartment beneath one of the lab tables. Inside, he discovered a journal filled with cryptic notes and sketches. As Jack pored over the journal, a pattern began to emerge. The Sleepy Smoke was not a mere accident or a product of nature.

It was a carefully concocted formula, designed to induce a deep slumber and manipulate the minds of those exposed to it. The journal hinted at a secret organization known as "The Order of Shadows," whose members sought to control the town of Sleepy Hollow and use the Sleepy Smoke to their advantage. They had infiltrated every aspect of the town, from the local government to the police force.

Realizing the magnitude of the threat, Jack knew he couldn't face the Order of Shadows alone. He sought the help of a few trusted allies – a brilliant chemist, a skilled hacker, and a fearless journalist. Together, they formed a secret alliance to bring down the Order and expose their evil plans to the world.

As they delved deeper into the investigation, they discovered that the Order had a hidden lair deep within the nearby forest. Armed with their collective skills and unwavering determination, they prepared for a final showdown. Under the cover of darkness, Jack and his team infiltrated the Order's lair. They faced numerous obstacles and traps, but their unwavering resolve pushed them forward.

The echoes of their footsteps reverberated through the dimly lit corridors as they closed in on the heart of the Order's operations. Finally, they reached the inner sanctum, where the leaders of the Order of Shadows awaited. A fierce battle ensued, with Jack and his team fighting against the Order's loyal followers. It was a battle of wits, strength, and sheer determination.

After a lot of struggle, Jack won. The leaders of the Order were apprehended, their plans thwarted. The town of Sleepy Hollow was finally free from the clutches of darkness. As the sun rose over Sleepy Hollow, a new era began. Jack and his team were hailed as heroes, their names etched in the town's history.

The Sleepy Smoke became nothing more than a distant memory, a reminder of the resilience of the human spirit and the power of unity. Jack knew that his work was not done. There were still mysteries to unravel and villains to apprehend. But as he looked out over the town he had saved, he couldn't help but feel a sense of pride and accomplishment. Sleepy Hollow would forever be grateful for the bravery of a detective who refused to give up, even in the face of darkness.

CHAPTER SEVEN

SHADOWS OF DECEPTION

Swift Smith was a seasoned private investigator, renowned for his unwavering determination and relentless pursuit of the truth. He had solved countless cases, but none had prepared him for the web of deceit that would consume his every waking moment.

It all began when Swift received a mysterious package at his office. Inside was a cryptic note and a photograph of a woman - Sophia Smith. The note read, "They're coming for her. Save Sophia before it's too late."

Intrigued and concerned, Swift delved into the mysterious world surrounding Sophia Smith. He discovered that she was a brilliant scientist working on a groundbreaking energy project, rumored to be capable of revolutionizing the world. But her research had attracted the attention of powerful entities, willing to go to any lengths to possess her knowledge.

Swift's investigation led him to a secret organization known as "The Consortium." They operated in the shadows, manipulating governments and corporations for their own gain. Swift uncovered a sinister plot involving the Consortium's desire to control Sophia's research and use it as a weapon.

Determined to protect Sophia, Swift reached out to her, warning her of the danger that lurked in the shadows. Reluctantly, she agreed to meet him, and they formed an unlikely alliance.

As they dug deeper, their lives were constantly under threat. Assassins lurked in the shadows, ready to eliminate anyone who stood in the Consortium's way. Swift and Sophia had to rely on their wits, resourcefulness, and an unbreakable bond to stay one step ahead.

The duo uncovered a trail of corruption that extended far beyond what they had anticipated. High-ranking government officials, influential businessmen, and even trusted allies were entangled in the Consortium's web of deception. The more they uncovered, the more dangerous their journey became.

With each step, Swift and Sophia grew closer, not only in their pursuit of the truth but also in their hearts. The pressure and constant danger forged a deep connection between them, and they found solace in each other's presence amidst the chaos.

One stormy night, as they were poring over documents in Swift's office, a sudden explosion rocked the building. The Consortium had found them. Swift and Sophia barely had time to react before masked assassins burst into the room. Gunfire erupted, and chaos ensued. Swift pushed Sophia to the floor, shielding her from bullets as they exchanged fire.

Using their training and instincts, Swift and Sophia managed to fend off their attackers, but they knew this was just the beginning. They had to find a safe place to regroup and plan their next move.

With the help of an old friend, a hacker named Max, they discovered a hidden safehouse on the outskirts of the city. It was a secluded cabin nestled deep within a dense forest, far away from prying eyes. Here, they could gather their thoughts and devise a strategy to take down the Consortium once and for all.

In the sanctuary of the safehouse, Swift and Sophia pored over the evidence they had gathered, connecting the dots and unraveling the Consortium's intricate network. They discovered that the energy project Sophia had been working on had the potential to solve the world's energy crisis. The Consortium, however, sought to monopolize this breakthrough technology and control the energy market, amassing unimaginable wealth and power.

As Swift and Sophia prepared to expose the Consortium's crimes, they realized they needed concrete evidence to bring them down. They decided to infiltrate the Consortium's heavily guarded headquarters, a towering skyscraper that stood as a symbol of their dominance.

Disguised as employees, Swift and Sophia made their way through the labyrinthine corridors, evading security cameras and patrolling guards. Their hearts raced as they approached the Consortium's high-security vault, where the evidence they sought was rumored to be stored.

Using their combined skills, Swift and Sophia bypassed the state-of-the-art security systems and accessed the vault. Inside, they discovered a trove of incriminating documents, detailing the Consortium's illegal activities, bribery, and manipulation of governments.

Just as they were about to leave, an alarm blared throughout the building. They had been discovered. Swift and Sophia raced against time, their hearts pounding as they fought their way through waves of armed guards.

Bullets whizzed past them, but their determination fueled their every move.

Finally, they reached the rooftop, where a waiting helicopter would be their ticket to freedom. But as they emerged onto the helipad, they were met with a shocking sight. The Puppetmaster, the enigmatic leader of the Consortium, stood before them, a malicious smile playing on his lips.

"You thought you could stop us?" he sneered. "You're too late."

With a wave of his hand, armed guards surrounded Swift and Sophia. The Puppetmaster reveled in their despair, relishing the moment of victory.

But Swift, fueled by his unwavering determination, refused to back down. He fought with everything he had, taking down guard after guard. Sophia, not one to be underestimated, used her scientific knowledge to create makeshift weapons, aiding Swift in their desperate struggle.

In a heart-stopping climax, Swift and Sophia confronted the Puppetmaster. It was a battle of wills, strength, and determination. With their lives hanging in the balance, they fought against overwhelming odds to expose the Consortium's crimes and save humanity from their malevolent grasp.

In a final act of desperation, Swift managed to overpower the Puppetmaster, disarming him and delivering a knockout blow. The Consortium's leader lay defeated at their feet.

As they stood on the rooftop, the wind whipping through their hair, Swift and Sophia knew that their mission was complete. The Consortium had been dismantled, and justice had been served. But the scars of their ordeal would forever remain. Their lives had been forever changed by the shadows of deception they had dared to confront.

As they parted ways, Swift and Sophia knew that their journey was not over. They had witnessed the true face of evil, and they vowed to continue fighting for justice, no matter the cost. Their bond, forged in the crucible of danger, would endure, and they would forever be connected by the shadows they had overcome.

Months later, Swift received a call from Sophia. She had taken refuge in a remote location, continuing her scientific research in secret. The world had yet to fully grasp the magnitude of the Consortium's crimes, and Sophia knew that she had to keep her work hidden until the truth could be revealed.

Swift agreed to meet her, eager to see her once again. As he made his way to the secluded location, he couldn't help but reflect on the journey they had embarked upon. The dangers they faced, the lives they saved, and the love that had blossomed amidst the chaos.

When Swift arrived, he was greeted by Sophia, her eyes filled with determination and hope. She revealed to him the progress she had made in her research, the potential to change the world for the better. She knew that their fight was not over, that they had to ensure the Consortium's influence was eradicated completely.

With renewed purpose, Swift and Sophia pledged to continue their mission, no longer as mere individuals but as a formidable force against corruption and deception. They knew that the shadows would always be there, ready to engulf the world. But armed with the truth and their unwavering resolve, they were determined to shine a light that would guide humanity towards a brighter future.

CHAPTER EIGHT

THE MOONLIGHT ESCAPE

It was a dark and stormy night. Susan, a young woman with a passion for adventure, found herself in a precarious situation. She had been hiking in the dense forest when a sudden downpour forced her to seek shelter in an abandoned cabin.

As she stepped inside, the door creaked ominously. The cabin was dilapidated, with cobwebs hanging from the ceiling and a musty smell permeating the air. Despite the eerie atmosphere, Susan felt relieved to have found refuge from the storm.

However, her relief quickly turned to fear when she heard a low, guttural growl coming from a hidden corner of the room. Trembling, she cautiously approached the source of the sound and discovered a trapped wolf, injured and frightened.

Susan's heart went out to the creature. With great caution, she approached it, speaking in soothing tones. The wolf seemed to sense her kindness and allowed her to examine its wounds. Determined to help, Susan fashioned a makeshift bandage from her torn shirt and gently tended to the wolf's injuries.

As the storm raged on, Susan realized that her only chance of survival was to escape the cabin. She couldn't shake the feeling that something sinister was lurking in the shadows, watching her every move.

With the wolf by her side, she devised a plan. Using her backpack and a rope she found, Susan created a makeshift grappling hook. She knew that the only way out was through the cabin's small attic window.

As she climbed the rickety stairs to the attic, the sound of footsteps echoed below. Panic surged through Susan's veins as she realized she was not alone. Someone or something was in the cabin with her.

With adrenaline coursing through her, Susan pushed open the attic window and threw the grappling hook onto a sturdy branch outside. The wolf followed suit, leaping through the window with surprising agility.

Just as Susan was about to make her escape, a figure emerged from the shadows below. It was a man, clad in tattered clothes, his eyes filled with madness. He lunged towards Susan, his intentions clear.

Summoning every ounce of courage, Susan fought back, using her survival instincts to defend herself. With the wolf at her side, she managed to fend off the crazed man long enough to make her daring escape.

As they ran through the forest, the storm finally began to subside. Susan and the wolf found themselves in a clearing, surrounded by the comforting glow of the moonlight.

Exhausted but determined, Susan realized that she had survived the nightmarish ordeal. She looked at the wolf, grateful for its unexpected companionship and protection.

With a newfound strength, Susan made her way back to civilization, vowing never to forget the power of courage and resilience. The cabin, haunted by its dark secrets, became a distant memory, a reminder of the strength she had found within herself.

And so, Susan continued her adventures, forever grateful for the moonlit escape that had shaped her into the fearless woman she had become.

Susan emerged from the forest, her heart pounding with a mix of adrenaline and relief. The storm had finally subsided, leaving behind a calm night illuminated by the soft glow of the moon. She looked at the wolf, who had become her loyal companion throughout the harrowing ordeal. Together, they ventured towards a nearby road, hoping to find help.

As they walked along the deserted road, a car approached in the distance. Susan waved her arms frantically, hoping to catch the attention of the driver. The car slowed down, and a kind-faced woman rolled down the window.

"Are you okay? Do you need help?" the woman asked, concern evident in her voice.

Susan, out of breath but grateful, explained her terrifying experience in the cabin and how the wolf had come to her aid. The woman listened attentively, her eyes widening with each detail.

"I can't believe what you've been through," the woman said. "I'm a wildlife rehabilitator, and I've been tracking a pack of wolves in this area. They're usually quite shy and avoid humans. It seems this particular wolf sensed your distress and chose to protect you."

Susan was amazed by the revelation. The wolf had not only saved her life but had also shown a level of compassion and intelligence that she had never witnessed before. She thanked the woman for her insight and asked if there was a nearby shelter where the wolf could receive proper care.

The woman offered to take them to a nearby sanctuary, where injured and orphaned animals were rehabilitated and released back into the wild. Susan agreed, knowing it was the best chance for the wolf to heal and return to its natural habitat.

At the sanctuary, Susan and the wolf were greeted by a team of dedicated professionals who assessed the animal's injuries. They assured Susan that with proper treatment and care, the wolf would have a good chance of recovery.

Susan spent the next few days volunteering at the sanctuary, helping the staff with various tasks. She learned about the importance of wildlife conservation and the struggles these creatures faced in the modern world.

During her time there, Susan developed a deep bond with the wolf. She named him Luna, in honor of the moonlight that had guided them through their escape. Luna's injuries gradually healed, and Susan witnessed his transformation from a wounded creature to a majestic symbol of resilience.

As Luna regained his strength, the sanctuary prepared for his release back into the wild. Susan knew it was time to say goodbye to her companion, as Luna belonged in his natural habitat.

On the day of Luna's release, Susan stood at the edge of a vast forest, her heart filled with bittersweet emotions. She watched as Luna bounded into the wilderness, his wild spirit once again unleashed.

With tears in her eyes, Susan whispered, "Thank you, Luna, for saving me and reminding me of the power of courage and compassion. You will forever hold a special place in my heart."

As Luna disappeared into the dense forest, Susan felt a sense of fulfillment. She had embarked on a simple hike that had turned into an extraordinary journey of survival, friendship, and personal growth.

From that day forward, Susan dedicated herself to wildlife conservation, using her experience and knowledge to raise awareness and protect the creatures she had come to cherish. She would forever be grateful for the moonlit escape that had not only changed her life but had also ignited a passion that would shape her future.

And so, Susan continued her adventures, forever carrying Luna's spirit within her, and vowing to make a difference in the world, one step at a time.

THE HAUNTED CABIN

Once upon a time, in a small village nestled deep within the woods, there stood an old cabin. It had been abandoned for years, with rumors of haunting and strange happenings surrounding it. Curiosity got the better of a young couple named Jack and Emily, who decided to explore the cabin one moonlit night.

As they approached the cabin, a chilling wind blew through the trees, making them shiver. The door creaked open as they cautiously entered. The air inside was thick with an eerie silence. Jack's heart raced as they ventured further into the dimly lit cabin.

Suddenly, a door slammed shut behind them. Panic filled the room as they realized they were trapped. A sense of foreboding crept over them, and they knew they were not alone. Shadows danced on the walls, and whispers echoed through the cabin, sending shivers down their spines.

Emily's trembling hand reached out to grasp Jack's as they explored the cabin, searching for a way out. They stumbled upon an old journal, its pages yellowed with age.

As they read the entries, their eyes widened with horror.

The journal belonged to a former resident of the cabin, who had dabbled in the dark arts. It spoke of a malevolent spirit that possessed the cabin, feeding off the fear of those who entered. The only way to escape its clutches was to solve a riddle hidden within the cabin's walls.

Determined to escape, Jack and Emily scoured the cabin for clues, their hearts pounding with each step. They discovered a hidden passage behind a bookshelf, leading them to a secret room. In the center of the room, a pedestal held a small, ornate box.

Inside the box, they found a note that read, "To escape this haunted place, find the key to the spirit's embrace." Confused, they searched the room for any sign of a key. Suddenly, Jack noticed a painting on the wall.

He carefully adjusted the painting, revealing a hidden compartment. Inside, they found a small golden key. With trembling hands, they approached the door that had trapped them and inserted the key into the lock. The door swung open, and they were free.

As they stepped outside, the moon emerged from behind the clouds, casting an ethereal glow on the cabin. They looked back one last time, feeling a mixture of relief and trepidation. The haunted cabin would forever remain etched in their memories, a reminder of the supernatural forces that lurked in the shadows.

And so, Jack and Emily walked away, hand in hand, vowing to never again venture into the realm of the unknown. Little did they know, the spirit of the cabin watched from within, awaiting its next victims.

Days passed, and the haunting memories of the cabin lingered in Jack and Emily's minds. They couldn't shake off the fear that had consumed them during their encounter with the malevolent spirit. Nightmares plagued their sleep, filled with visions of the haunted cabin and the dark presence that lurked within.

One evening, a knock on the door startled them. Jack cautiously opened it, revealing a weathered old man named Samuel. He had a haunted look in his eyes, mirroring the fear that Jack and Emily had experienced.

"I used to live in that cabin," Samuel whispered. "I managed to escape its clutches, but the spirit followed me, tormenting my every step."

Jack and Emily exchanged worried glances, realizing that their encounter with the cabin had awakened something dark within them, connecting them to the spirit's wrath.

Samuel explained that the only way to break free from the spirit's grip was to find an ancient object hidden deep within the forest. Legend had it that this object possessed the power to banish the spirit forever.

Driven by desperation, the trio embarked on a perilous journey, battling through dense foliage and overcoming numerous obstacles. The forest seemed to come alive, its branches reaching out like twisted fingers, attempting to ensnare them.

After what felt like an eternity, they stumbled upon a hidden clearing. In the center stood an ancient stone pedestal, adorned with intricate carvings. Samuel recognized it as the resting place of the object they sought.

With trembling hands, they found a small recess in the pedestal, perfectly shaped to fit the golden key they had discovered in the cabin. As they turned the key, the ground rumbled beneath them, and a blinding light engulfed the clearing.

When their vision cleared, they fond themselves back at the cabin. But something was different. The air felt lighter, and the once ominous atmosphere had dissipated. The spirit was gone.

Filled with relief, Jack, Emily, and Samuel returned to the village, sharing their harrowing tale with the villagers. The haunted cabin became a distant memory, a cautionary tale passed down through generations.

As for Jack and Emily, the experience had changed them, leaving them with a newfound appreciation for the balance between light and darkness, and a deeper understanding of the power of the human spirit to overcome even the most malevolent forces.

And so, they lived out their lives, cherishing each moment and forever grateful for the strength they had found within themselves. The haunted cabin had taught them the true meaning of courage and resilience, a lesson they would never forget.

CHAPTER TEN

THE GIFTED JOURNEY

Once upon a time, in the quaint town of Willow Creek, a young woman named Emma discovered she possessed a remarkable gift – the ability to see and communicate with spirits. This extraordinary power had been passed down through generations in her family, originating from her renowned psychic grandmother. However, Emma had kept her secret hidden, fearing the judgment and disbelief of others.

One fateful day, Emma's life took an unexpected turn. She received a mysterious letter, elegantly scripted, which simply stated, "I know your secret. Meet me at midnight in the old abandoned mansion on the outskirts of town." Intrigued and apprehensive, Emma's curiosity got the better of her, and she resolved to uncover the truth behind the enigmatic message.

As midnight approached, Emma cautiously approached the decrepit mansion. The moon's full glow cast an eerie light upon the crumbling walls, while the wind whispered through the trees, heightening the sense of foreboding. With a racing heart, Emma stepped inside, guided by an unseen force through the dark corridors.

Finally, she arrived at a room at the end of the hallway. The door creaked open, revealing a shadowy figure seated in a worn chair. "Emma," the figure spoke in a low, raspy voice. "I've been waiting for you."

Emma's breath hitched in her throat. Though unfamiliar, there was an inexplicable familiarity surrounding the figure. Trembling, she managed to inquire, "Who are you?"

The figure chuckled darkly. "I am Tyson, your grandmother's former apprentice. She kept my existence hidden from you, for she knew the perils that accompany your extraordinary abilities."

Emma's mind swirled with questions, but before she could voice them, Tyson continued, his voice laced with intrigue. "I have been observing you, Emma. Your gift is rare, and with my guidance, we can unlock its true potential. Together, we can become unstoppable."

Conflicted by fear and curiosity, Emma hesitated for a moment before cautiously agreeing to Tyson's proposal. Over the following weeks, he became her mentor, teaching her the art of controlling her abilities, communing with spirits, and even manipulating the living world. Emma's powers flourished, growing stronger with each passing day, and a newfound sense of invincibility coursed through her veins.

Yet, as Emma delved deeper into the supernatural realm, she uncovered a malevolent secret. Tyson harbored a hidden agenda. He desired to exploit her powers for his own gain, seeking to manipulate both the living and the dead to satisfy his twisted desires.

Realizing the deception, Emma knew she had to confront Tyson to prevent him from unleashing havoc upon the world. She devised a plan, choosing to face him in the very mansion where their paths first crossed. Steeling herself, she understood that she must utilize her powers to defeat him and protect those she held dear.

The night of the confrontation arrived, and Emma stood resolute in the grand foyer of the mansion. Her heart pounded, a mix of fear and determination coursing through her veins. Emerging from the shadows, Tyson appeared with a sinister smile on his face, taunting her with his superiority.

"You thought you could outsmart me, Emma?" he sneered. "You are nothing compared to my power."

Emma, having learned from her past mistakes, had grown stronger in both her abilities and her resolve. Summoning every ounce of energy within her, she focused it into a potent burst of light, directing it directly at Tyson.

The force of her blast knocked Tyson off his feet, sending him crashing into a nearby wall. Emma stood tall, her eyes glowing with newfound strength. She had triumphed over the darkness that threatened to consume her.

With Tyson defeated, Emma realized the weight of her responsibility. She vowed to utilize her gift for the greater good, becoming a renowned psychic who used her abilities to help others find closure and peace. She never forgot the valuable lessons learned or the perils that lurked within the shadows.

As time passed, Emma's story transformed into a legend within Willow Creek. Whispers of the girl who conversed with spirits, the girl who confronted darkness and emerged victorious, echoed through the town. Despite the unimaginable challenges she faced, Emma embraced her gift as an integral part of her identity, committed to using it to illuminate the world and banish the shadows of doubt and fear.

With Tyson defeated, Emma emerged from the abandoned mansion, her heart overflowing with a mix of relief and triumph. The moon bathed her in its gentle glow, as if celebrating her victory. As she made her way back to town, a newfound sense of purpose filled her being. She knew she had a responsibility to use her gift wisely and protect the innocent from the darkness that lurked.

Word of Emma's extraordinary abilities spread throughout Willow Creek like wildfire. People sought her out for guidance, desperate to connect with loved ones who had passed away or seeking closure for unresolved matters. Emma embraced her role as a psychic, dedicating herself to helping those in need.

But as her reputation grew, so did the demand for her services. Emma soon found herself overwhelmed by the constant stream of visitors seeking her assistance. Determined not to let her gift become a burden, she sought the guidance of her grandmother's old journals.

Within the pages of the journals, Emma discovered ancient rituals and techniques that could enhance her abilities and provide her with the clarity she sought. She devoted herself to studying and perfecting these methods, honing her skills to become an even more powerful psychic.

Emma also realized that she needed a sanctuary, a place where she could retreat from the demands of the world and recharge her energy. She found solace in a hidden cabin deep within the woods surrounding Willow Creek. The cabin had belonged to her grandmother, and it held a sense of tranquility and familiarity that she cherished.

Within the walls of the cabin, Emma created a sacred space where she could meditate, commune with spirits, and delve into her psychic abilities without distractions. Surrounded by nature's serenity, she felt connected to a higher power, guiding her on her journey.

As Emma's reputation continued to grow, so did the challenges she faced. Dark forces, envious of her power and influence, sought to undermine her and discredit her abilities. Rumors and skepticism spread like a poisonous vine, threatening to tarnish her reputation.

Undeterred, Emma remained steadfast in her mission. She knew that the true power of her gift lay not in convincing skeptics, but in bringing comfort, healing, and closure to those who believed in her. With every successful reading, she restored faith in the unseen and reminded the world of the interconnections of life and death.

However, there was one particular challenge that tested Emma's resolve like never before. A grieving mother, desperate to reconnect with her deceased child, sought Emma's help. The pain in the mother's eyes was palpable, and Emma could not turn her away.

Using her enhanced abilities, Emma delved deep into the spiritual realm, searching for a connection to the child's spirit. But as she reached out, an unexpected darkness enveloped her. A malevolent force seized upon her vulnerability, threatening to consume her light.

Emma's heart raced as she battled against the darkness. She drew upon her inner strength, the lessons learned from her grandmother, and the love she held for humanity. With sheer determination, she broke free from the clutches of the malevolent force, her spirit shining brighter than ever before.

The mother's tears turned to tears of gratitude as Emma relayed messages from her child. The connection forged in that moment was more profound than Emma could have imagined. It reminded her of the immense responsibility she carried and the impact she could have on people's lives.

As time passed, Emma's abilities continued to evolve. She began to see glimpses of the future, offering guidance and foresight to those who sought her counsel. She also discovered the power of energy healing, using her touch to soothe physical and emotional ailments. Through her gift, she became a beacon of hope and a catalyst for transformation.

But amidst the accolades and successes, Emma never lost sight of the delicate balance between her gift and the world around her. She remained humble, grounded, and grateful for the opportunity to make a difference. Her encounters with darkness had taught her the importance of vigilance and discernment, ensuring that she used her powers for good and never succumbed to the temptations that awaited her.

Years passed, and Emma's legacy became intertwined with the fabric of Willow Creek. She became a revered figure, not only for her psychic abilities but also for her unwavering compassion and integrity. People from far and wide sought her guidance, and even skeptics found solace in her presence.

As Emma grew older, she knew it was time to pass on her knowledge and gift to the next generation. She sought out young individuals who exhibited the same potential and guided them with the wisdom she had accumulated over the years. She nurtured their abilities, teaching them the importance of responsibility and the need to protect the delicate balance between the physical and spiritual realms.

Emma's final years were spent in peaceful seclusion, surrounded by the love and gratitude of those she had helped. She passed away peacefully, her spirit ascending to a realm where her gift would forever shine.

Her legacy lived on, echoing through the generations that followed. The story of Emma, the gifted psychic who unveiled the shadows, became a timeless tale of courage, resilience, and the power of embracing one's unique abilities.

And so, in Willow Creek, the legend of Emma remained etched in the hearts of its people, a testament to the extraordinary power that lies within each of us and the potential we hold to bring light to the darkest corners of the world.

Emma's journey would forever serve as a reminder that within every challenge lies an opportunity for growth, and that even in the face of darkness, the light of our inner gifts can guide us to the path of true purpose and fulfillment.

CHAPTER ELEVEN

THE BOOK OF SCARY TOWNS

Once upon a time, Sam the explorer reached the gates of magic library, he curiously entered and took a book, 'The Book of Scary tows'. The book contained hundreds of stories about forbidden towns, as he flipped pages and read, he got to know that the world is filled with darkness.

He read the first chapter,

"Long ago, nestled deep within the dark and foreboding woods, there stood a village known as Ravenshade. It was a place shrouded in mystery and whispered tales of horror. The villagers who resided there lived in constant fear, for their lives were plagued by a sinister presence that lurked within the very fabric of the village itself.

Legend had it that Ravenshade was once a thriving community, prosperous and full of life. But one fateful night, a powerful curse befell the village, casting it into eternal darkness. The curse was said to be the work of a vengeful witch, whose wrath was unleashed upon the unsuspecting villagers after they had wronged her.

The witch, known as Morana, had been an outcast within the village, feared and ridiculed for her strange abilities and unsettling appearance. She had sought solace in the depths of the forest, where she delved into the forbidden arts of dark magic, harnessing the very essence of evil itself.

Driven by her desire for revenge, Morana concocted a wicked spell that would forever bind the village to her malevolent will. Under the cover of night, she sneaked into the heart of Ravenshade, placing a cursed talisman within the village square. As the moon reached its zenith, the curse took hold, enveloping the village in an eternal night.

From that moment onwards, Ravenshade became a place of perpetual darkness, where the sun never rose and the moon cast an eerie glow upon the twisted trees. The once vibrant and cheerful streets were now desolate and haunting, haunted by the tormented spirits of those who had perished under Morana's curse.

As the years passed, the village fell into disarray. The curse had not only trapped the villagers in perpetual darkness but had also twisted their souls, turning them into monstrous beings consumed by their own fear and despair. They became the very embodiment of the curse, their bodies contorted and their minds lost to madness.

The few survivors who remained in Ravenshade lived in constant fear, barricading themselves within their crumbling homes, praying for salvation that never came. They whispered stories of the witch's curse, warning outsiders to stay away, for anyone who dared to enter the village would be forever trapped within its nightmarish grasp.

Ravenshade became a forbidden place, its name whispered in hushed tones by those who dared to speak of it. The forest surrounding the village grew thicker and more impenetrable, as if nature itself was trying to shield the world from the horrors that lay within. Generations passed, and the tales of Ravenshade became mere folklore, a cautionary tale to scare children into obedience. But the village remained, its cursed existence a dark stain upon the land. The souls trapped within its boundaries cried out in anguish, their tortured wails carried on the cold wind that swept through the desolate streets.

As time wore on, rumors spread of brave souls who dared to venture into the cursed village. They were drawn by the allure of uncovering the truth behind the witch's curse and seeking to break its hold upon the land. But each expedition ended in tragedy, their fates sealed by the malevolent forces that guarded the secrets of Ravenshade.

Whispers of a secret artifact, hidden deep within the village, began to circulate among those who sought to unravel the mysteries of Ravenshade. It was said to hold the key to breaking the curse, a glimmer of hope in the darkness that consumed the village.

But no one had ever returned with the artifact, their bodies lost forever within the cursed boundaries of Ravenshade. Legends spoke of a chosen one, a hero destined to free the village from its eternal torment. It was said that this hero would possess a pure heart and unwavering courage, capable of facing the horrors that awaited within Ravenshade. But as the curse grew stronger, hope dwindled, and the legend of the chosen one became nothing more than a whisper in the wind.

The village itself seemed to feed upon the fear and despair of its inhabitants, evolving into a living nightmare. The twisted trees reached out with gnarled branches, their skeletal fingers clawing at the villagers who dared to venture outside. Shadows danced along the streets, whispering sinister promises and luring the unsuspecting deeper into the heart of darkness.

The once lively homes and shops of Ravenshade now stood as decrepit shells, their walls covered in layers of dust and cobwebs. The air was thick with a suffocating silence, broken only by the occasional creak of a rotting floorboard or the distant howl of a tormented soul. It was a place frozen in time, forever trapped within the grasp of its own malevolence.

But even in the darkest of nights, hope flickered like a dying flame. There were those who refused to abandon Ravenshade to its cursed fate, determined to uncover the truth and bring an end to the suffering. They formed a secret society, known as the Order of the Raven, dedicated to studying the curse and finding a way to break it. The members of the Order risked their lives, delving into forbidden texts and ancient rituals, desperate to unlock the secrets that bound Ravenshade.

They were guided by fragments of forgotten prophecies and cryptic symbols, piecing together a puzzle that had plagued the village for centuries. Their efforts were not in vain, for within the hidden depths of the village, they discovered a hidden chamber. In its center lay an ornate pedestal, upon which rested the artifact they had sought for so long.

It was a small, glowing crystal, pulsating with an otherworldly energy. The legends had been true - this crystal held the power to break the curse. With trembling hands, the chosen member of the Order lifted the crystal from its resting place. The moment the artifact was removed, a surge of energy rippled through Ravenshade. The darkness trembled, fighting against its impending demise.

But the light of the crystal grew stronger, illuminating the village with a radiant glow. As the curse was shattered, the souls of the villagers were finally set free from their tormented existence. The sun, long forgotten, began to rise over Ravenshade, casting its warm rays upon the once cursed land. The twisted trees straightened, their branches reaching towards the light, as if embracing a newfound freedom.

Ravenshade, no longer a place of nightmares, slowly began to rebuild. The villagers returned, their hearts filled with gratitude and a newfound appreciation for the light that had been absent for so long. The village thrived once more, its streets bustling with life and laughter, forever grateful for the heroes who had shattered the curse that had plagued them for generations.

But the legend of Ravenshade would never be forgotten. It served as a reminder of the darkness that lurks within the human heart and the consequences of unchecked vengeance. The village stood as a testament to the resilience of the human spirit, a beacon of hope in a world where darkness always threatens to consume."

Shivers sent down the spine as Sam read this. But, he thought that, "As being as a explorer, I must not stop learning." This made him read another chapter.

"Once upon a time, in a small town nestled deep within the misty mountains, there existed a scary and long backstory that had been passed down through generations. The townsfolk would gather around the flickering fireplaces, their eyes wide with anticipation, as the elderly storytellers would begin to weave their tales.

Legend had it that centuries ago, the town was plagued by a malevolent sorcerer named Malachi. He was said to possess dark powers that could bend reality itself. Malachi's reign of terror was marked by his insatiable thirst for power and his desire to control the town and its inhabitants.

The townspeople, fearing for their lives, sought the help of a wise old witch named Elara. She was known for her vast knowledge of ancient spells and enchantments. Elara devised a plan to defeat Malachi, but it required the combined efforts of the entire town.

Under the cover of darkness, the townsfolk gathered at the edge of the forest, armed with courage and determination. Elara led them through a treacherous journey, filled with perilous traps and enchanted creatures. They faced their deepest fears and overcame countless obstacles, all in the hope of freeing their town from Malachi's clutches.

Finally, after what felt like an eternity, they reached the heart of the forest, where Malachi's lair lay hidden. The air crackled with magic as Elara chanted ancient incantations, summoning the forces of light to aid them in their battle.

The townspeople fought valiantly, their swords clashing against Malachi's dark magic. The battle raged on for hours, but in the end, the combined strength of the townsfolk proved too much for the sorcerer. Malachi was defeated, his powers stripped away, and he was banished from the town forever.

However, the victory came at a great cost. The town had suffered immeasurable losses, and the scars of the battle would forever be etched into their hearts. To honor the fallen heroes, the townspeople erected a grand monument in the center of the town, a symbol of their resilience and unity.

From that day forward, the town thrived, its people living in peace and harmony. The story of their triumph over evil became a cautionary tale, a reminder of the strength that lies within a community when faced with adversity.

And so, the scary and long backstory of the town became a cherished part of their history, passed down from one generation to the next. It served as a reminder that even in the face of darkness, hope and bravery can prevail, and that the power of unity can conquer any foe."

The book didn't end there, it had lot more stories and Sam continued to read them,

"Once upon a time, there was a small town in the middle of a large forest called, Sun Valley. It had been built many years ago, when its inhabitants were full of life and hope of a prosperous future. But then, something strange began to happen.

One day, the people of Sun Valley noticed a mysterious fog slowly circling around their village. Nobody knew where it had come from and everyone was scared. The fog felt almost tangible, like a presence in the air that embraced the town in its eerie embrace.

As days passed by, the whole town became consumed by this strange fog. It felt like everyone was in a living nightmare and no one was really asleep. The fog shrouded the town and the people in a kind of darkness and gloom.

Although the people of the village tried to go about their day-to-day lives, they were all filled with an unspoken dread that something was coming. Even though the people of Sun Valley had no reason to think this, something inside of them told them it was true.

In the middle of the night, strange screams could be heard coming from the forest. Nobody knew what they were, but they scared everyone that heard them. People didn't dare to venture out into the darkness and so nobody knew the reason for these cries of terror.

One day, the screams stopped and it didn't take long for people to realize that something was wrong in the village. Nobody knew what had happened, but something had changed, the feeling of dread became worse and people started to become paranoid.

It was then that the stories began to spread. Stories of the monsters that lived in the forest, stories of people being taken away in the night. Every morning, more people would be missing, leaving behind their belongings as they were taken away by an unknown force.

As more people disappeared, the few that were left behind became desperate and the whole town felt doomed. People stopped coming into the village and the town slowly became a ghost town.

After what felt like a long time of living in fear of the monsters, a mysterious hero finally arrived in Sun Valley and help rid the village of the strange fog and monsters.

Finally, the people of Sun Valley could rest easy and live happily again. Yet, even as the town recovered, the people never stopped looking over their shoulder, always aware that danger might come back once more."

Then he read more,

"In the heart of the Appalachian Mountains, nestled between dense forests and winding rivers, lies a small town called Millfield. It's a place that seems to be frozen in time, with its old-fashioned storefronts and cobblestone streets. But beneath its charming exterior lies a dark and haunting history that has left the townspeople living in fear.

Millfield was founded in the late 1800s by a group of settlers who were drawn to the area's natural beauty and fertile soil. They built their homes and businesses along the banks of the nearby river, and for a time, life was good. But as the years passed, strange things began to happen. At first, it was just rumors and whispers. People spoke of strange noises in the night, of shadows moving in the darkness. Some claimed to have seen ghostly figures lurking in the woods, while others reported feeling an icy chill run down their spines when they passed by certain houses.

But as the stories grew more frequent and more terrifying, it became clear that something truly sinister was at work in Millfield. The first real tragedy struck in 1912, when a young girl named Ophelia disappeared without a trace. Her parents searched high and low for her, but she was nowhere to be found. Days turned into weeks, and weeks turned into months, until finally, Ophelia's body was discovered in a nearby cemetery. She had been brutally murdered, her throat slashed from ear to ear. The town was thrown into a state of panic.

Who could have done such a thing? Was it a wild animal? A deranged stranger? Or was it something more sinister? The police launched an investigation, but they came up empty-handed. The case went cold, and Ophelia's killer was never brought to justice.

But that wasn't the end of Millfield's troubles. Over the years, there were countless other disappearances and murders, each one more gruesome than the last. Some victims were found with their throats slashed like Ophelia's, while others were found with their bodies twisted into unnatural positions or covered in strange symbols. It seemed as though there was a serial killer on the loose, preying on the town's unsuspecting residents.

The police tried their best to catch the culprit, but they were always one step behind. Witnesses reported seeing a shadowy figure lurking in the darkness, but when they tried to pursue him, he vanished into thin air. It was as though he had supernatural powers at his disposal.

As the body count rose and fear gripped the townspeople like a vice, rumors began to circulate about a curse that had befallen Millfield. Some said that it was punishment for the sins of its founding fathers, who had stolen land from the local Native American tribes without permission or compensation. Others claimed that it was retribution for the way that Millfield had treated its outcasts and misfits over the years, driving them out of town and leaving them to fend for themselves in the wilderness.

Whatever the cause may be, it's clear that Millfield is cursed. The townspeople live in constant fear of what might happen next, never knowing when or where the next victim will strike. Some have even begun to believe that there's no escaping the curse - that it's woven into the very fabric of Millfield itself, an unbreakable bond that will keep them trapped here forevermore. But despite all this darkness and despair, there are still glimmers of hope in Millfield. There are people who refuse to give up or give in to fear - people who are determined to uncover the truth about what's really going on in their town and put an end to the madness once and for all"

And so, the next story began,

"The town of Helmsville was once a quaint and peaceful place. Everyone knew each other and the town was relatively happy and prosperous. But something had changed, and no one was sure what it was.

It began with a series of strange occurrences. People would report hearing strange noises coming from the woods at night and seeing mysterious lights flickering in the distance. People began to get scared and rumors started circulating around town that something strange was going on.

The townspeople's fears were soon confirmed when a group of children went missing from the town. Their parents had gone searching for them, but all their efforts were in vain. No matter how hard they looked, they couldn't find the kids.

Then, one night, a group of children returned to the town. But something was off about them. They were pale, their eyes were glazed over, and they seemed to be in a trance. It was as if something had taken control of them.

The children had strange stories to tell about what had happened to them. They said that a mysterious being had taken them to a place deep within the woods, and forced them to do horrible things. They had been terrorized and threatened with death if they ever tried to leave.

The townspeople were horrified by the children's tales and began to wonder what could be lurking in the woods. They decided to send a group of brave men into the woods to investigate.

The men soon came upon a small cabin deep in the woods and inside, they found a woman. She introduced herself as Lilith and claimed that she was the one responsible for the strange events. She had used dark magic to take control of the children and was using them to do her bidding.

The townspeople were stunned by her admission and decided to take her back to the town. They put her in a cell and barred the door, but Lilith seemed unfazed. She just smiled and said there was no escape from her dark power.

The townspeople were determined to put an end to Lilith's reign of terror and, with the help of a powerful witch, they were able to create a magical barrier around the town that Lilith couldn't penetrate.

But the townspeople weren't out of danger yet. Lilith had created an army of undead creatures and sent them out to attack the town. Despite the magical barrier, the creatures were still able to get through and cause chaos and destruction.

It was then that a young girl named Sara stepped forward. She had been secretly studying magic and had a plan to defeat Lilith's forces. With the help of the townspeople, Sara was able to cast a powerful spell that destroyed the undead creatures and banished Lilith from the town.

Sara was hailed as a hero and, with the help of the townspeople, was able to restore peace and prosperity to Helmsville"

And so, went the next chapter,

"Once upon a time, nestled deep within the misty mountains, there lay a town named Melcoda. The townsfolk whispered tales of a curse that had befallen their ancestors centuries ago. Legend had it that a powerful sorcerer had once resided in the town, using his dark magic to control the minds of the people. But one fateful day, the townsfolk rose up against him, banishing him to the depths of the nearby forest.

However, the sorcerer's curse lingered, casting a shadow over the town for generations to come. The once vibrant and prosperous community became isolated and shrouded in mystery. The townsfolk, fearing the sorcerer's return, erected a towering stone wall around their beloved home, sealing themselves off from the outside world.

As the years passed, the town became a place frozen in time. The buildings, with their weathered facades, stood as a testament to the town's rich history. The streets, once bustling with laughter and life, now echoed with an eerie silence. The townsfolk, bound by tradition and superstition, adhered to strict rules and rituals passed down through the generations.

Children grew up hearing stories of the sorcerer's dark powers, and the fear of his return became ingrained in their very souls. The town's elders, the keepers of the ancient knowledge, taught the young ones to be vigilant, to never venture beyond the town's protective walls.

But one day, a young girl named Amelia, with her insatiable curiosity and adventurous spirit, dared to question the town's traditions. She yearned to uncover the truth behind the sorcerer's curse and bring light back to her beloved town.

Amelia delved into the town's archives, poring over dusty tomes and deciphering cryptic symbols. She discovered a hidden passage in an ancient book that spoke of a long-lost artifact, said to hold the key to breaking the curse. Determined, she embarked on a perilous journey through the forbidden forest, braving its treacherous paths and facing her deepest fears.

After days of searching, Amelia stumbled upon a hidden cave, its entrance guarded by ancient runes. With trembling hands, she deciphered the symbols and entered the cavern. Inside, she found the artifact, a shimmering crystal pulsating with untold power.

With the artifact in her possession, Amelia returned to the town, her heart filled with hope. She gathered the townsfolk, who had long forgotten the taste of freedom, and shared her discovery. Together, they formed a plan to break the curse once and for all.

Under the light of a full moon, Amelia and the townsfolk gathered at the heart of the town. With the artifact held high, she chanted the ancient incantation passed down through generations. The crystal glowed brighter and brighter until a blinding light engulfed the town.

When the light faded, the townsfolk found themselves standing outside the walls they had called home for so long. The curse had been broken, and the town was free once more. Joyful laughter filled the air as the townsfolk embraced their newfound freedom, their spirits lifted from the weight of the past.

And so, the town with its scary, different, and long backstory became a place of wonder and enchantment. The walls that had once kept them safe now stood as a reminder of their resilience and the power of unity. From that day forward, the town flourished, its people embracing change and embracing the world beyond their walls, forever grateful to the brave young girl who had brought light back to their lives."

The book came to an end, but Sam's curiousity. He embarked on a quest to uncover the truths. He would experience experiences that he would remember forever.

CHAPTER TWELVE

ELDORIA'S MYSTERIES

In the remote village of Eldoria, nestled deep within the misty mountains, a dark secret lay hidden. Few ventured into the village, for its eerie atmosphere and whispered tales of supernatural occurrences kept most at bay. But one man, the renowned investigator Draven Nightshade, was drawn to Eldoria like a moth to a flame.

Draven Nightshade was a master of the occult, with a reputation for unraveling the most perplexing mysteries. His sharp mind and unwavering determination had earned him the moniker of "The Enigma Solver." When he heard of the strange happenings in Eldoria, he knew he had to investigate.

Upon his arrival, Draven sensed an otherworldly presence, an ancient evil that lurked beneath the surface. The villagers, gripped by fear, spoke in hushed tones about a malevolent force known as the Shadow Weaver, a wicked sorcerer who had cursed Eldoria centuries ago.

Draven sought the assistance of the village elder, a wise and enigmatic woman named Seraphina Moonshadow. Seraphina was the guardian of Eldoria's ancient archives, holding the knowledge of generations past. She revealed that the only way to break the curse and banish the Shadow Weaver was to find the Tears of Elysium, a set of mystical gemstones imbued with pure light.

Driven by a sense of duty and armed with the wisdom of Seraphina, Draven embarked on a perilous journey to locate the Tears of Elysium. His first destination was the forgotten city of Zephyria, said to be the resting place of the first gemstone.

Deep within the ruins of Zephyria, Draven discovered a hidden chamber, adorned with cryptic symbols and ancient artifacts. As he deciphered the engravings, he realized that the gemstone was guarded by a formidable creature known as the Draconian Serpent.

Undeterred, Draven confronted the serpent, engaging in a battle of wits and skill. With each strike, the serpent grew more enraged, unleashing its fury upon Draven. But he remained steadfast, using his knowledge of ancient spells and his quick reflexes to outmaneuver the creature. In a final act of bravery, Draven struck the serpent's vulnerable spot, defeating it and claiming the first Tear of Elysium.

With the first gemstone in his possession, Draven continued his quest, journeying to the enchanted forest of Lumina. There, he encountered a mystical guardian named Aria Whisperwind, a skilled archer with a mysterious past. Aria revealed that the second Tear of Elysium was hidden within the heart of a treacherous labyrinth, guarded by the spirits of fallen warriors.

Together, Draven and Aria ventured into the labyrinth, facing numerous trials and tribulations. They encountered vengeful apparitions, illusionary traps, and the echoes of battle. Draven's expertise in the occult and Aria's unparalleled archery skills proved crucial as they navigated the labyrinth's treacherous passages.

After what felt like an eternity, they reached the heart of the labyrinth. There, they faced the spirits of the fallen warriors, who challenged them to a duel. With each strike of their weapons, the spirits grew stronger, fueled by their desire for vengeance.

Draven and Aria fought valiantly, their determination unwavering. They utilized their unique talents, combining their magical prowess and archery skills to overcome the spectral warriors. In a climactic moment, Draven unleashed a powerful spell, banishing the spirits and claiming the second Tear of Elysium.

With two Tears of Elysium in his possession, Draven knew he was one step closer to breaking the curse. He returned to Eldoria, where Seraphina awaited him with grave news. The Shadow Weaver had unleashed his minions upon the village, spreading chaos and despair.

Driven by a sense of urgency, Draven and Aria joined forces with Seraphina and the remaining villagers to defend Eldoria. The battle was fierce, as the Shadow Weaver's minions unleashed their dark magic upon the village. Draven and Aria fought side by side, their combined powers creating a shield of light that repelled the darkness.

In the midst of the chaos, the Shadow Weaver revealed himself—a sinister figure with glowing crimson eyes and a malevolent aura. Damien Voss, as he was known, had once been a respected sorcerer, but his thirst for power had corrupted him, leading him down a path of darkness.

A climactic battle ensued between Draven and Damien, their powers clashing in a cataclysmic display of light and shadow. The fate of Eldoria hung in the balance as the two sorcerers fought for control. Draven, fueled by his determination to protect the innocent, summoned the power of the Tears of Elysium.

The gemstones glowed with an intense radiance, enveloping Draven in a brilliant aura. With a surge of energy, he unleashed a wave of pure light that shattered Damien's dark magic. The Shadow Weaver, weakened and defeated, vanished into the depths of the village, never to be seen again.

Eldoria was saved, and the curse was finally broken. The villagers rejoiced, grateful for Draven's bravery and Aria's skill. Seraphina, with tears of joy in her eyes, thanked Draven for his unwavering resolve and the sacrifices made to save their village.

As the sun set over Eldoria, Draven and Aria bid farewell to the villagers, their mission fulfilled. They knew that their paths would cross again in the future, as new mysteries awaited them both. They vowed to continue their fight against darkness and protect those in need, their bond forged through the trials they had overcome.

And so, Draven Nightshade and Aria Whisperwind ventured into the unknown, their names destined to become legends whispered in the shadows. Their adventures would continue, as they sought to bring light to the darkest corners of the world, forever bound by their shared quest for truth and justice.

As the new adventurers entered the ancient gates of Eldoria, they were greeted by an ethereal presence. The air hummed with an otherworldly energy, and the city seemed to come alive with whispers of forgotten tales.

Seeking answers, the group stumbled upon an ancient library nestled within the heart of Eldoria. Dusty tomes lined the shelves, their pages filled with forgotten knowledge. A worn leather-bound book caught their attention, titled "Chronicles of Eldoria: A History Unveiled."

Eager to uncover the secrets of Eldoria's past, they opened the book and began to read the faded pages. The words told a story of a land once teeming with magic, where mythical creatures roamed freely and the power of the elements was harnessed by its inhabitants.

Eldoria, the book revealed, was founded by a group of powerful sorcerers known as the Eldorians. Gifted with extraordinary abilities, they built the city as a haven for all who sought to study and master the arcane arts. The city flourished under their guidance, becoming a beacon of knowledge and enlightenment.

But as time passed, a darkness began to seep into Eldoria. The Eldorians, consumed by their own ambitions, grew divided. The pursuit of power corrupted some, leading to conflict and chaos that threatened to tear the city apart.

In their final act of desperation, the Eldorians made a pact with the ancient spirits of Eldoria, binding their powers and sealing them away to protect the city from destruction. The spirits, in turn, infused their essence into the very fabric of Eldoria, ensuring its preservation and safeguarding their knowledge for future generations.

The adventurers were awestruck by the revelation, understanding that the city they now stood in was not just a physical place but a living embodiment of the Eldorians' sacrifice and the spirits' guardianship.

Driven by a newfound purpose, the group delved deeper into the library, unearthing long-forgotten prophecies that foretold of a chosen few who would come to Eldo ria in its time of need. They were destined to rekindle the dormant magic within the city, heal the divisions that plagued its people, and restore Eldoria to its former glory.

Armed with this knowledge, the adventurers set out on a quest to unite the scattered remnants of the Eldorians' power. Each fragment they found would not only grant them greater mastery over magic but also bring them closer to unlocking the true potential of Eldoria itself.

Their journey would be perilous, testing their resolve and challenging their understanding of the world. They would encounter ancient guardians, solve riddles left by the Eldorians, and confront their own inner demons. But with each step forward, they would uncover forgotten truths, heal the scars of the past, and pave the way for a brighter future for Eldoria.

And so, the adventurers ventured forth, their hearts filled with the weight of Eldoria's history and the hope of a new era. Guided by the knowledge they had unearthed, they would breathe life back into the forgotten magic of Eldoria, reignite the spirits that dwelled within, and forge a destiny that would forever change the fate of this mystical city.

About The Author

From an aspiring to an award winning author, Stavya Garg's love for storytelling knows no bounds. Born on 08th July 2012, from a very young age, Stavya has been captivated by the power of words and their ability to transport readers to different worlds. With a vivid imagination and a passion for creating captivating narratives, they (Stavya and his power of words) embarked on a writing journey to share their stories with readers of all ages.

Inspired by renowned authors Ruskin Bond and Chetan Bhagat, Stavya's writing style is a unique blend of mystery, adventure, and relatable characters. Their debut book showcase their ability to craft suspenseful plots that keep readers eagerly turning the pages, while also presenting relatable characters that resonate with audiences.

While this is Stavya's first published work, their dedication to the craft of writing is evident in every word they pen. They have honed their skills by attending workshops conducted by Chetan Bhagat, where they gained valuable insights into the art of storytelling. Additionally, reading books such as "Musoorie Mystery" by Ruskin Bond has broadened their horizons and provided them with a deeper appreciation for the wonders of mystery and adventure.

Beyond his writing endeavors, Stavya is an avid reader who delves into various genres, always seeking new authors and fresh perspectives. This curiosity and love for literature serve as a constant source of inspiration, fueling their creativity and pushing the boundaries of their storytelling.

With their debut book, Stavya marks the beginning of what promises to be an exciting literary journey. Their dedication, passion, and talent shine through in every page, leaving readers eager to see what they will create next. As they continue to explore the realms of imagination, Stavya is already planning their next project—a novel that will transport readers to new worlds and captivate them with imaginative storytelling. Stay tuned for more captivating stories from this young author as Stavya's literary journey unfolds, leaving a lasting impact on readers worldwide.

Hope you liked the book,

Its great that you have read the book till now,
so,

Thank You !

Hope you loved the thrillers I wrote.

www.ingramcontent.com/pod-product-compliance
Lightning Source LLC
Chambersburg PA
CBHW020628160726
47991CB00002B/948